Good Meat Makes Its Own Gravy

Be Blessed!
Rev. Walter Thomas

But strong meat belongeth to them
that are of full age, even those
who by reason of use have their senses
exercised to discern both good and evil.

—Hebrews 5:14, KJV

Good Meat Makes Its Own Gravy

135 SERVINGS FOR THE SOUL

WALTER S. THOMAS
Compiled and Edited by Allison Elizabeth Brown

Judson Press, Valley Forge

Good Meat Makes Its Own Gravy: 135 Servings for the Soul
© 2000 by Judson Press, Valley Forge, PA 19482-0851

Library of Congress Cataloging-in-Publication Data

Thomas, Walter S.
    Good meat makes its own gravy : 135 servings for the soul / Walter S. Thomas ; compiled and edited by Allison Elizabeth Brown.
    p. cm.
    ISBN 0-8170-1388-1 (pbk. : alk. paper)
1. Sermons, American--20th century. I. Brown, Allison Elizabeth. II. Title.
BV4253 .T544 2000
252--dc21   00-060209

Printed in Canada
06 05 04 03 02 01 00
10 9 8 7 6 5 4 3 2 1

Contents

Foreword

Have you ever been in a situation where you just needed a word, a thought, an idea, a suggestion, a key that could inspire you to hold on, to fight on? If you have, then these words of Dr. Walter S. Thomas in this work, *Good Meat Makes Its Own Gravy*, are an answer to prayer.

In this work, you will find words of encouragement that will help you to understand that God is relevant, caring, and liberating when you keep the faith. When you read this work, you will gain insights that will help you understand how to get the best out of your relationship with God and people. The book will also give you vital instructions on how to enter spiritual warfare and come out of it victoriously.

Walter Thomas is one of the nation's premier preachers. In this book he shares with the reader some compelling and astute sayings that will give you "strength for the journey." Dr. Thomas's wit, wisdom, and faith will draw you in and not release you until you reach the final page. Without a doubt, this book is a fantastic read!

Bishop John R. Bryant
Presiding Prelate, 10th District
African Methodist Episcopal Church, Dallas, Texas

Preface

HOW THIS BOOK CAME TO BE

It is a terrible thing to be hungry and not fed. It is also a terrible thing to be fed but not given exactly what you need in order to become a strong, healthy person. The fact is, most malnourished people eat something. Unfortunately, these persons are never satisfied because the food is neither sufficient nor nutritious and well-balanced. Thus, these malnourished individuals drift here and there, getting a morsel whenever they can, wherever they can, despite the kind of food or its condition. The same is true for many who seek to grow in a relationship with God.

When I came to New Psalmist Baptist Church in Baltimore, Maryland, back in 1996, I was, in fact, both hungry and malnourished. I loved the Lord but was not getting enough nutrition in my spiritual diet to be victorious in my everyday life. Then I heard the Word. So wonderful was this Word, so healing was this Word, that I began to feel the torn places in my life mend, the cobwebs in my mind clear, and my vision become more focused. No longer was I wasting away on mere milk, but my soul began feasting on succulent meat that was tender enough to digest, understand, and apply to my everyday life. No longer was I starving, but with each serving, I saw myself, as well as my loved ones who attended service, become strengthened and fulfilled. I started taking notes simply to retain the life-changing knowledge of the Word. Little did I know then what God had in mind!

Good Meat Makes Its Own Gravy has been a labor of love and appreciation. Inspired by the Holy Spirit, the book was compiled as a gift, in honor of the twenty-fifth pastoral anniversary of Dr. Walter S. Thomas. Each excerpt is a powerful chunk of God's wisdom, taken from various sermons I've heard over the past four years of my membership at New Psalmist Baptist Church. I asked God to supply me with a unique way to express my sincere gratitude to my pastor for the awesome way in which he has been used to influence my spiritual walk. *Good Meat Makes Its Own Gravy* is the manifestation of God's answer to that request!

It is time for many of us to go from milk to meat in the body of Christ. Jesus said, "Man cannot live by bread alone." I have come to understand that he meant we also need the good meat of God's Word, often spoken to us by his "handpicked" servants, in order to thrive and realize our God-given potential. It is my prayer as you partake of and savor each morsel contained in this book that your soul will be strengthened as mine has been.   —Allison Elizabeth Brown

Acknowledgments

First, I want to thank New Psalmist Baptist Church and my family for receiving these words of faith with enthusiasm. This work would never have come to pass without the enthusiasm of Allison Brown. She took notes each week and presented this "gift of words" on my twenty-fifth pastoral anniversary. Thanks also to Brother Odell Dickerson, who worked personally with me through the process of bringing this project to formal publication. Thanks for keeping me on track! Thanks, too, to Judson Press and its editors for accepting this work and seeing its value for the wider community. Finally, thanks to God for the words that are included here, for they really belong to him. He loaned them to me for sermons. —WST

To the Father, Son, and Holy Spirit, whose companionship and instruction is unparalleled, thank you for doing "Exceedingly, abundantly beyond what I could ask or think." Special thanks to Pastor Thomas and the first family, for being exactly who you are...the best is yet to come! Also to Judson Press, thank you for grabbing hold of the vision and partnering with us to bring it to fruition. Last but certainly not least, to my loving and supportive family and church family, thanks for everything! Remember: "Eyes have not seen...."   —AEB

IN THE BEGINNING, GOD ...

Genesis 1:1a

Serving *1

When understanding God know ...

God deals in free fall.
You can't hold on to where you
have been and still expect to go
where God is taking you.

Serving *2

When understanding God know ...

God gives us time that we waste, but we never give God time that he wastes.

Serving *3

When understanding God know ...

The kingdom of God is the reign of God in your heart. The kingdom has to be something you want.

Serving *4

When understanding God know ...

God does the calling, but *you* do the choosing.
God calls you, but then *you* have
to choose whether you want to go God's way.

Serving *5

When understanding God know ...

God never forgets when
you choose him.

Serving *6

When understanding God know ...

Your competence is not the issue.
Your submission is.

Serving *7

When understanding God know ...

In a relationship with God,
obedience *is* submission.

Serving *8

When understanding God know ...

If you want to be free and delivered,
then God's way is the only way.

Serving *9

When understanding God know ...

You need to live your life with a fiery desire to do something for God.

WITHOUT FAITH ...

Hebrews 11:6

Serving *10

When maturing in faith know ...

Acts of faith must always be individualized.

Serving *11

When maturing in faith know ...

Faith's explanations always come later.

Serving *12

When maturing in faith know ...

Faith is not about what I know,
but about who God is.

Serving *13

When maturing in faith know ...

K
nowledge is gas.
Faith is the engine.

Serving *14

When maturing in faith know ...

What I believe about my life is a direct reflection of what I believe about God.

Serving *15

When maturing in faith know ...

History does not have to repeat itself!
If we can't change, then every word
of the gospel is a lie.

Serving #16

When maturing in faith know ...

If I want to go deeper with God,
I must rethink what is possible.

Serving *17

When maturing in faith know ...

In order to be a cut above the rest, you have to move from passive faith to productive faith.

Serving *18

When maturing in faith know ...

There is some stuff God does not let you know. But what God does reveal, God knows you can handle.

Serving *19

When maturing in faith know ...

When you don't know
what to do, hope!

ISSUES AND STRUGGLES ...

Ephesians 6:12

Serving *20

When dealing with issues and struggles know ...

Get today straight *first*.

Serving *21

When dealing with issues and struggles know ...

It was something natural that *hurt* you, but you need something supernatural to *heal* you.

Serving *22

When dealing with issues and struggles know ...

God does not have any spiritual hemophiliacs.
If you bleed, you will clot.

Serving *23

When dealing with issues and struggles know ...

When God delivers you,
elevate your vision.

Serving *24

When dealing with issues and struggles know ...

God chose you 'cause God wants others
to see what can be done with rejected people!

Serving *25

When dealing with issues and struggles know ...

Ninety percent of our problem is that we try to bring the old "us" into the new challenge.

Serving *26

When dealing with issues and struggles know ...

If God can order the seasons
and all of nature, can't God also
maintain order in your life?

Serving *27

When dealing with issues and struggles know ...

We have called weakness
in ourselves what God has called
wickedness in humanity.

Serving *28

When dealing with issues and struggles know ...

God delivers *from* sin,
not *in* sin.

Serving *29

When dealing with issues and struggles know ...

In the conversations of emotionally wounded persons, you can hear the absence of their inner wholeness.

Serving *30

When dealing with issues and struggles know ...

Sick people make other people sick.

Serving *31

When dealing with issues and struggles know ...

Self-esteem is a part of
the gift of salvation.

Serving *32

When dealing with issues and struggles know ...

Involve yourself in
something significant.

Serving *33

When dealing with issues and struggles know ...

God cannot use you for great service until you've experienced great suffering.

Serving *34

When dealing with issues and struggles know ...

With God—
no matter how bad it gets—
it's still good!

Serving *35

When dealing with issues and struggles know ...

You've got to know the difference between *objective* goals and *subjective* desires.

Serving *36

When dealing with issues and struggles know ...

Many Christians are saved—
but confused.

Serving *37

When dealing with issues and struggles know ...

God took your confusion into consideration when he established the plan for your future.

Serving *38

When dealing with issues and struggles know ...

Great growth will come from great grief. If you find yourself in the midst of great trials, it's because there is going to be great growth.

Serving *39

When dealing with issues and struggles know ...

Any chaos in your life
has been deemed by God to be either
allowable or necessary.

Serving *40

When dealing with issues and struggles know ...

We are surprised when
we mess up—but God is not.

Serving *41

When dealing with issues and struggles know ...

The only way not to have bad memories
is not to have bad deeds.

Serving *42

When dealing with issues and struggles know ...

God didn't save you to make you perfect.
... God saved you to make you righteous.

Serving *43

When dealing with issues and struggles know ...

Perfection deals with deeds; righteousness deals with my relationship to God.

Serving *44

When dealing with issues and struggles know ...

As you grow, the nature of
your stumbling block changes to match
the height God is taking you to.

Serving *45

When dealing with issues and struggles know ...

Stumbling helps you see other people differently. You begin to understand how easy it is for someone else to fall.
You gain compassion.

Serving *46

When dealing with issues and struggles know ...

The church has to be
a place where
stumbling people are welcome.

Serving *47

When dealing with issues and struggles know ...

When you stumble, you learn something about God that only people who've fallen know.

Serving *48

When dealing with issues and struggles know ...

We cannot handle the pressure of being all God wants us to be all the time.

Serving *49

When dealing with issues and struggles know ...

You will be deceived if you think you will
make it to glory without struggle.

Serving *50

When dealing with issues and struggles know ...

Folks don't wanna struggle through nothing!

Serving *51

When dealing with issues and struggles know ...

When issues arise, we get caught up
in the issue and forget about the mission.

Serving *52

When dealing with issues and struggles know ...

The longer you cry over spilt milk,
the more derelict you become
with your responsibilities.

Serving *53

When dealing with issues and struggles know ...

Failure does not disqualify you
from the blessings of God.

Serving *54

When dealing with issues and struggles know ...

Diseased means dis-eased—not at ease.

Serving *55

When dealing with issues and struggles know ...

God wants to take care of you and heal you in his secret place so that you are at ease and others are not dis-eased. God is setting you apart so that others don't get diseased.

Serving *56

When dealing with issues and struggles know ...

There's no such thing as God healing you
over and over for the same thing.
If you are still suffering from the same illness,
it is for one of two reasons:

Serving *56 continued

#1 You didn't get rid of all of
it the first time—because as usual
you didn't take all of your prescription
the way you were supposed to!
#2 You were reinfected.

Serving *57

When dealing with issues and struggles know ...

Just because you've been healed doesn't mean you don't have scars. ... But I'd rather have scars than be bleeding and wounded any day!

Serving *58

When dealing with issues and struggles know ...

*P*urpose is one
of our biggest issues.

Serving *59

When dealing with issues and struggles know ...

Whoever said learning only includes
the positive? God allows failure to be
a teacher in our lives.

Serving *60

When dealing with issues and struggles know ...

If you've got to break down,
break down in front of God and not
in front of people.

Serving *61

When dealing with issues and struggles know ...

God will remove the "down" from "breakdown" and replace it with "through" or "out."

Serving *62

When dealing with issues and struggles know ...

The steps and stops of a good person
are ordered by the Lord.

Serving *63

When dealing with issues and struggles know ...

Ever thought about how many more mistakes you and I would make if Christ weren't there?

WARFARE AND WICKEDNESS ...

2 Corinthians 10:4

Serving *64

When confronting warfare and wickedness know ...

The adversary's ultimate agenda
is to steal our praise.

Serving *65

When confronting warfare and wickedness know ...

The territory you're in is
not strange to God.
He wants you to depend on him.

Serving *66

When confronting warfare and wickedness know ...

God speaks to you first.
Then the enemy comes
with plausible alternatives.

Serving *67

When confronting warfare and wickedness know ...

When you know the days are evil,
you know the truth will be distorted.

Serving *68

When confronting warfare and wickedness know ...

Not all your enemies are outside your camp. Some are inside your camp.... Some are inside you.

Serving *69

When confronting warfare and wickedness know ...

You know there is a monkey on your back
when people, in general, become a burden
to you. Then you know something
has hold of your spirit.

Serving *70

When confronting warfare and wickedness know ...

You know there is a monkey on your back
when you have internalized the warfare—
to the extent that the warfare is no longer just
a battle but your normal condition.

Serving *71

When confronting warfare and wickedness know ...

You know there is a monkey on your back
when you're talking more about the hell
in your face than the heaven in your life.

Serving *72

When confronting warfare and wickedness know ...

$top believing the enemy's lies.

Serving *73

When confronting warfare and wickedness know ...

Ain't nothing evil leavin' until *you* put it out.

Serving *74

When confronting warfare and wickedness know ...

When God is doing something,
you have to have someone in your space
who has confidence in it.

Serving *75

When confronting warfare and wickedness know ...

If you don't deal with your history,
your history will deal with you.

Serving *76

When confronting warfare and wickedness know ...

There's a war going on between those who want God and those who don't want God. Like it or not, you are involved.

Serving *77

When confronting warfare and wickedness know ...

There is a rope-a-dope strategy
in the spirit realm.

Serving *78

When confronting warfare and wickedness know ...

All the enemy has to
work with is illusion.

Serving *79

When confronting warfare and wickedness know ...

The enemy is banking on the fact that you and I will accept his lies.... The biggest lie we buy into is, "This is just the way I am."

Serving *80

When confronting warfare and wickedness know ...

All sins are committed when we buy into Satan's lies.

Serving *81

When confronting warfare and wickedness know ...

It is in darkness that we discover the light of God.

Serving *82

When confronting warfare and wickedness know ...

The sword of the Spirit is only as good
as the hand that holds it.

Serving *83

When confronting warfare and wickedness know ...

In any battle, a good run beats
a bad stand any day.

Serving *84

When confronting warfare and wickedness know ...

Deceptive leaders will have
you going places you
don't need to go.

Serving *85

When confronting warfare and wickedness know ...

There is always an angelic announcement before the move of God. He never blindsides you.

Serving *86

When confronting warfare and wickedness know ...

Knowing where you've been will help you stay where you are, so you can get to where you need to be.

Serving *87

When confronting warfare and wickedness know ...

The enemy is out
to kill your witness.

Serving *88

When confronting warfare and wickedness know ...

Your witness is your ability to be who you are despite your circumstances—and only God can give you that peace and that power.

Serving *89

When confronting warfare and wickedness know ...

God has a witness protection program!

Serving *90

When confronting warfare and wickedness know ...

When we ask, "Why do the wicked prosper?"
we are envying those who have
no promise of security and protection.

Serving *91

When confronting warfare and wickedness know ...

Some forces won't bother you
'cause they don't want what's in you
to deal with them.

Serving *92

When confronting warfare and wickedness know ...

When it comes to adversity,
God will let "much" come against us,
but not "too much"!

Serving *93

When confronting warfare and wickedness know ...

Sin will always put you
in a strange land.

Serving *94

When confronting warfare and wickedness know ...

The adversary does all he can to stop
us from enjoying God.

Serving *95

When confronting warfare and wickedness know ...

ou have to take it by force,
'cause you lost it by fear.

Serving *96

When confronting warfare and wickedness know ...

"No weapon formed against me shall prosper"
is a *rhema* word. It is context specific. It is not
a promise just for any Christian. It is for the
weary, shamed, fallen, abused, hopeless,
the crying.... This is your new life guarantee.

RELATIONSHIPS ...

1 John 4:18

Serving *97

When growing in relationships know ...

Never expect people to treat you better than they treat God.

Serving *98

When growing in relationships know ...

Men: Listen to her.
Her heart needs to come out,
and she needs to know it's been heard.

Serving *99

When growing in relationships know ...

Women: He defines love as admiration. To be loved is to be admired, so admire him.

Serving *100

When growing in relationships know ...

Don't make others pay for what *you* picked up in your past relationships.

Serving *101

When growing in relationships know ...

Marriage is both a J-O-Y and a J-O-B.
You have to decide what day of the week
you add your Y or B to the JO.

Serving #102

When growing in relationships know ...

Everybody is following somebody.
Be careful to whom you give the
privilege of leadership.

Serving #103

When growing in relationships know ...

If your marriage is in trouble,
first ask yourself, "Am I whole?"

Serving *104

When growing in relationships know ...

Love will get you in trouble when relating to the opposite sex is one of the undisciplined areas of your life.

Serving *105

When growing in relationships know ...

Love will get you in trouble when you have never been taught how to love yourself.

Serving *106

When growing in relationships know ...

When you do not love yourself,
you will begin to lust for love.

MORE WISDOM ...

Proverbs 4:5—7

Serving *107

When seeking more wisdom know ...

Until you accept the truth,
you will never be free.

Serving *108

When seeking more wisdom know ...

"Grace = God's riches at
Christ's expense."...
And he paid full price for it.

Serving *109

When seeking more wisdom know ...

Sometimes the greatest help you can give folks is to leave them alone.

Serving *110

When seeking more wisdom know ...

Disobedience put us into bondage; obedience is the only way out!

Serving *111

When seeking more wisdom know ...

Part of the problem in the church is that we have a lot of active people with no orders from God.

Serving *112

When seeking more wisdom know ...

Many people in the church
apply for positions that
the Spirit has not declared "vacant."

Serving *113

When seeking more wisdom know ...

When the Bible says, "Judge not," what it means is, "Do not attach some ultimate reality to that which you see because God can change anything."

Serving *114

When seeking more wisdom know ...

Jealousy is "I want what you have."
Envy is "I want to be you."

Serving *115

When seeking more wisdom know ...

"Redeeming the time" means taking advantage of every opportunity that comes your way to exhibit and exemplify the power of Jesus Christ in your life.

Serving *116

When seeking more wisdom know ...

"Will" and "walk" go together.
But you don't discover "will" until you've
been walking a while.

Serving *117

When seeking more wisdom know ...

There is a direct correlation between your walk and your understanding.... The reason most folks can't understand their purpose is that they are walking in a direction different from where the understanding is to be found.

Serving *118

When seeking more wisdom know ...

Book knowledge is not a substitute for relationship and revelation.

Serving *119

When seeking more wisdom know ...

Where you go for your spiritual bread must be consistent with your value system.

Serving *120

When seeking more wisdom know ...

There may come a time when you must change churches.

Serving *121

When seeking more wisdom know ...

Good meat makes its own gravy.

ALWAYS GO BACK TO GOD ...

Revelations 1:11

Serving *122

When understanding God know ...

There is always good news when you hang close to God.

Serving *123

When understanding God know ...

The moment you start confessing your sin,
God starts to remove the threat
of curse from you.

Serving *124

When understanding God know ...

God does not care what folks believe
about me. God cares about what
I believe about me.

Serving *125

When understanding God know ...

God gives you conviction.
The devil gives you guilt.

Serving *126

When understanding God know ...

Whenever leaders defy the order of God, they release chaos and confusion into the lives of those they oversee.

Serving *127

When understanding God know ...

God is going to do it!

Serving *128

When understanding God know ...

God blesses those who are intentional
about what they want.

Serving *129

When understanding God know ...

God gives us answers to every question.
We just have to discover them.

Serving *130

When understanding God know ...

Growth is never free. There are high costs for being all you want to be.

Serving *131

When understanding God know ...

Even though growth costs, the Lord
has a reimbursement plan.

Serving *132

When understanding God know ...

God has a divine continuum....
We have to wait for God to send us a
word that will link us to it.

Serving *133

When understanding God know ...

God is the great God of reversal.
He takes what was crushing you
and uses it to give you victory.

Serving *134

When understanding God know ...

God does something special for every generation—because the next generation cannot make it on the miracles of the last one. Not all of us are at the Red Sea. Some of us are at the Jordan.

Serving *135

When understanding God know ...

"They brought the sick out into the streets
and laid them on beds and couches,
that at least the shadow of Peter passing by
might fall on them" (Acts 5:15).
It's time to expect shadow power.